Capricorn Man in Love

How to Attract a Capricorn Man and Get Him to Fall in Love with You

by Eli Ansen

Table of Contents

Introduction

What do Edgar Allan Poe, Muhammad Ali, Richard Nixon, Elvis Presley, and Orlando Bloom have in common? Believe it or not, all of these successful men are Capricorns.

Throughout history, there have been a number of famous and successful people that were born under this astrological sign. It's not surprising because Capricorn men are known to be ambitious and dedicated to achieving success. They are goal-driven and they are most likely to reach the top in their chosen fields. They are also very loyal partners and are committed to their relationships. Falling in love with a Capricorn man can be the best thing for a woman looking for stability and true love. But what does it take to attract this kind of man and how can a girl make him fall in love with her?

For the longest time, folks have relied on their Zodiac signs for guidance on aspects of their lives such as love, relationships, careers, money, and so on. Many believe that with an accurate knowledge and interpretation of the stars, one can determine the course of their life and even possibly direct it down a more favorable path. Using their knowledge of

Astrology and the Zodiac signs, psychics have been able to determine and understand the personalities of people and have helped them redirect their lives. Compatibility, when it comes to friendships, romance, and business relationships are now easier to determine than ever before. Moreover, a love that's written in the stars may not be a fantasy after all.

The Capricorn man makes a good friend, lover, and business partner. With this book, you'll get to know more about men born from December 22 to January 19. Learn all about his personality, what he likes in women, and how you can make him notice you and fall deeply in love with you. If you already have a Capricorn man, then you'll get useful tips on how to make your relationship a happy and lasting one. Happy reading!

Chapter 1: Understanding the Capricorn Personality

The Capricorn man may look reserved and kind of hard to read but that doesn't mean that you have to be in the dark about what he likes and what he thinks. Here is a simple guide to understanding the personality of the Capricorn male.

Personality Trait 1: Goal-Oriented vs. No Ambition

The symbol for the Capricorn is a mythical creature - half-goat and half-fish. In understanding the Capricorn personality, you must know what the goat and the fish symbolize. The goat as a mountain climber represents the Capricorn's drive to succeed. It represents practicality, ambition, and the desire to rise. On the other hand, the fish represents emotions and contentment for a simple, uncomplicated life. In general, Capricorn males become successful in their chosen careers and they are often financially stable because of their ability to make practical decisions in life and their determination to achieve their goals. This happens when the person embraces the goat in him and leaves behind the fish. Then again, there are Capricorn men who remain fishes. These men have not yet decided what goals they want to pursue in life. They follow their emotions over practicality and they are happy to stay right where they are. As a result, these Capricorn males typically have financial problems and no career stability.

In case you meet a Capricorn who is still at this point in his journey, just remember that all Capricorns are born for greatness. He just needs more time to decide on his goals. Once he has decided, he will be on his way to success.

Personality Trait 2: Traditional vs. Unconventional

A lot of women enjoy going out with guys who have traditional values, who stick to the rules and play by the book. If you are among these women, then the Capricorn man is for you. The Capricorn male is very traditional when it comes to relationships. He can be very conservative and old-fashioned so if you are a girl with modern principles, then you might not hit it off with the Capricorn male.

The Capricorn man is set on his ways and he may not be too flexible when it comes to accepting new ideas and practices. Remember that this type of man is responsible, practical and levelheaded, so he understands that the tried-and-proven ways are the best ways of doing things. The adventurous type may find the Capricorn guy too boring to be with.

Conversely, the Capricorn man who is more in touch with his fish part rather than the goat part tends to be less sensible. He is more in touch with his emotions and so he can break free from tradition and even show bouts of eccentricity, especially when encouraged.

Personality Trait 3: Too Serious vs. Easy-going

Capricorn men work hard in order to attain the fulfillment of their ambitions. All too often, they become too focused on their goals that they lose the ability to have some fun in their lives. Many Capricorn men are so single-minded in their pursuit for success that they become too serious in life. They exhaust most of their time, energy, and attention on work and their career. As a result, the personal life of the Capricorn male may suffer. There is not much time for himself, friends, and relationships. He may not have time to engage in hobbies and cultivate his interests. He can become very unhappy, even when he attains career and financial success.

On the other hand, the Capricorn male who has not yet found his purpose in life can be very easy-going and can be a fun person to be with. He has no real concern for money or work so he is able to spend much of his time and energy on going out with friends and pursuing his interests. Needless to say, the Capricorn man who has learned to find balance between his work and personal life is the happiest.

Personality Trait 4: Cautious vs. Defiant

As mentioned, Capricorns are a traditional bunch and so they prefer to follow the safe route most of the time. And while it is true that they are driven when it comes to their ambitions, they will easily back away when they sense a possibility of failure. Capricorn men are not risk-takers. They will work hard for success but they will always take the path that will lead to sure success. When the Capricorn man reaches financial stability and he is contented with his career, he will stop there and will not make an effort to go further or reach higher. They consider this a safe place to be. Capricorns are cautious that way.

Conversely, the Capricorn who hasn't accepted their goat side will show defiance for their inner drive.

These Capricorn men will refuse to pursue goals and will give up easily when met with obstacles and pressures that they cannot handle. Their development as a full Capricorn is still premature and they have not yet made peace with the ambitious, goal-driven part of themselves.

Personality Trait 5: Pessimism and Attitude for Success

The Capricorn's drive to succeed is often based on his fear of being considered a failure. He holds other people's opinion of him in high regard and does not want to be regarded as a loser. Because of this kind of thinking, he is motivated to set goals, work hard for its attainment, and reach success.

One of the reasons why many Capricorns are successful is because of their pessimism. They always consider the negative side of things and work to prevent any of these from happening. It is the reason why many Capricorns strive to attain financial stability and career security. Because of this pessimism, the Capricorn becomes cautious about everything.

Personality Trait 6: Faithfulness vs. Duty

One cannot find a more loyal partner than a Capricorn male. Capricorns work hard to achieve success in any aspect of their life, whether it's about their career, finances, or romantic relationships. Perhaps, the reason lies in the Capricorn's sense of purpose when it comes to succeeding. They will certainly want to succeed in friendships, romantic, or business relationships.

Capricorns are loyal, faithful, and devoted to making their relationships, not only work, but more importantly - succeed. They will do whatever it takes to keep the relationship going. Unfortunately, many Capricorns will often lose sight of the real meaning of relationships. They can become mechanical and may keep their connections with other people out of duty.

Personality Trait 7: Self-Limiting vs. Achieving More

By now, you have a good idea about the male Capricorn's personality. He is an achiever and a go-getter, albeit he is cautious and traditional. Because of these qualities, the Capricorn male subconsciously puts a limit in what he can attain. In reality, the Capricorn male can probably go higher in life. He can achieve so much more than what he already has.

Many Capricorn male are content to be managers and supervisors, instead of being the CEO or the president of a company. They will stay with less than ideal friends and romantic partners because they imagine these to be "safe" and less risky. The Capricorn man will stay within safe borders rather than risk failing.

The Capricorn man has many good traits such as being steadfast when it comes to achieving his goals. He is loyal to his friends, girlfriend, wife, or business partner. Once he has embraced the goat in the Capricorn, there is nothing that will stop him from becoming successful in any aspect of his life, whether in relationships, money, or career. Conversely, he can be too pessimistic, conventional, and as a result, not a very fun person to be with.

Chapter 2: How to Attract a Capricorn Man

Now that you understand the personality of the Capricorn man, it is easier to catch his attention! Attracting the Capricorn man is easy with these very useful tips. And mind you, these are tricks that really work!

Step 1: Show Him that You Can Help Him Achieve His Goals

One of the surest ways to catch the attention of a Capricorn man is to show that you can help him attain success. Keep in mind that the Capricorn male values one important thing more than anything else - success. Due to this fact, he will most likely be attracted to someone who can help him advance in his career, earn more money, or improve his social status. If you are aware of his goals in life and you have some connections or means to make all of these goals happen, then don't hesitate to inform him. By doing so, you are sure to catch his attention.

Step 2: Be Open about Your Own Goals

Talk to him about your personal goals and how you are working hard to attain them. The saying, "Birds of the same feather, flock together," applies all the more in the case of the Capricorn man. He will most certainly be attracted to women who work hard and have definite goals in life. He feels that a woman who works hard for her goals is very much like him and if he has this kind of person by his side, his chances of succeeding will be doubled. Some men don't like listening to their woman talk about her goals, work, and career. It can be emasculating for many men to learn that the girl they are dating has ambitions of power, money, and success. But to the Capricorn man, a woman talking about her dreams to rise in life is the biggest turn on of all. So go on ahead and share your ambitions and your plans for success with him.

Step 3: Be Straightforward but Not too Forward

The Capricorn man is a no-nonsense guy. He is very practical and likes to be talked to in a straightforward manner. If you are attracted to him, it will help to just tell him about how you feel. However, remember that the Capricorn man is also conservative and traditional when it comes to courtship. The best way to tell him that you like him is to say it frankly without going around the bush. He will appreciate this but make sure that once you have told him about how you feel, never act too forward. This can turn him off. The Capricorn male likes to do things by the book so let him ask you out on dates, open doors for you, pay for meals, and leave the sexual advances to him.

Step 4: Talk Business and Culture

Although it doesn't sound like the normal courtship topic, Capricorn men are attracted to women who know about business and money. If you are wondering what topics of conversation can get a Capricorn man engaged, the answer is not flirting. Capricorn men dislike flirting or talking about trivial topics. Also, they don't enjoy flirting because it makes them feel embarrassed. Remember that Capricorns have a high regard for what other people think of them. Instead, if you really want to attract that handsome Capricorn, engage him in a conversation about business. He likes to talk and learn about business and anything that has to do with making money. He will consider you a knowledgeable person if you are well-versed with business terms and issues and he will definitely regard you as someone that can help him move forward. He also likes topics about culture, so gab away and share your extensive knowledge about philosophy, art, music, and literature. The Capricorn male appreciates people who are experienced and learned because he can always learn something from them.

As you can see, the Capricorn man is a special kind of guy. Unlike other men that initially fall for looks and female wiles, the Capricorn male prefers a woman who has goals and works hard for it. He wants a girl who is knowledgeable and has something to contribute in making him a better person.

Chapter 3: Making a Capricorn Man Fall in Love

So you've caught his attention, now what? Making the Capricorn man fall in love with you requires time and effort. However, once he has you in his heart, you will find that all of the time and energy that you've spent are well worth it. Here's how to make the Capricorn man fall head over heels for you.

Step 1: Make Him Feel Special

By this time, you and your Capricorn man are in the dating stage. Whether it's your first date or your third, there are some things that you need to do if you want him to fall hopelessly in love with you. For starters, you need to make the Capricorn male feel special. Tell him how you've never met anyone like him and how you've never seen things done as efficiently as he does it. He will consider these compliments and it help boost his ego. Always praise him for his achievements and comment positively on all his endeavors. Ask him about his projects and just listen and let him talk. He will interpret this as a sign of your interest for things he is passionate about. Whenever you need his advice, be sure to ask him for it. It makes him feel flattered that you consider his opinions and ideas useful information.

Step 2: Don't Rush It

Consider making a Capricorn man fall in love with you an investment. You'll need to give a lot of your time and energy in making it happen, but as soon as it does, you'll find that you are a very lucky woman. When making a Capricorn male fall in love with you, rushing things is not the way to go. You cannot put a time frame on it. This type of guy does not fall in love quickly. Bear in mind that the fully developed Capricorn man is a practical, levelheaded person. But If he is still more in touch with the fish part or the emotional part of being a Capricorn, then he can open up to another person much faster.

The Capricorn man is not quick to fall in love because of his cautious nature. Remember his fear of failure and his pessimism? All of these contribute to his inability to open his heart to a woman right away. He will need to do some pondering and when he's convinced that it is safe and that it is the right thing to do, then he will allow himself to fall in love with the girl he likes.

So to make a Capricorn man fall in love with you, take things slowly. Don't rush him into taking the next step in your relationship. Keep in mind that the Capricorn man can back out from an endeavor if he feels pressured. Be patient and just let things cook. When he is ready, he will tell you the words you want to hear and show you the love that you've been yearning for.

Step 3: Find a Way to Fit in His Future

It is important that you know your Capricorn man's goals and plans for the future. You will need to fit in it. The Capricorn man is determined to succeed in life. He wants to have a successful career and he wants to have financial stability. He will want someone that can stand by him and support him and his goals. If you are somehow wrong for his future, let's say, your own future plans will prevent him from attaining his goals, then he might not fall in love with you. Also, remember that the Capricorn is very traditional. That could mean that he would want to fall in love with a woman who has plans to start a family. If you want what he wants for the future, then make it known to him right away. Who knows, he and you could be making your future plans together right now!

At first, it all seems so difficult to attract a Capricorn man and make him fall in love with you. However, once you get in a relationship with this type of guy, you will be rewarded with the most dedicated, faithful, and loving partner.

Chapter 4: Building a Long-Lasting Relationship

You've diligently followed the advice in the previous chapters and now you and your Capricorn man are happily, deeply in love! Of course you'd want a long-term, fulfilling relationship! Don't worry; here are some tips you can follow to make sure that you keep your Capricorn man happy in your arms.

Step 1: Be 100% Committed to the Relationship

Women who are not ready to make a life-long commitment are not good partners for the Capricorn man. This guy wants stability in a relationship and he will only be in one that he thinks is for keeps. Capricorn men are the most dedicated and loyal partners. He will expect his girl to show the same kind of commitment that he gives in the relationship. If you are in a relationship with a Capricorn man, you should always express your seriousness for your future together. Always consider him when making plans for the future. Better yet, make your plans for the future together. He will see that you consider him to be an important part of your life.

The Capricorn man is an especially jealous guy. Some women try to make their man jealous just to shake things up, but this does not go down well with a Capricorn. It is not recommended to test his boundaries because he will just become disappointed and will feel hurt. Capricorn men need to feel that he is in a stable and solid relationship, without doubts and loopholes. Trust is a very important factor in every kind of relationship but for a Capricorn male, it is everything.

Step 2: Be Expressive of Your Support

The Capricorn man is very pessimistic. It's what drives him to succeed. But often, his negative feelings make him feel insecure and unsure of himself. A loving, supportive partner can help drive away all of his uncertainties about his skills and capabilities. A Capricorn male feels happy in a relationship where he feels the support of his partner. He will feel confident when he is assured that his girl will always be on his side, always there for him. The ideal partner for the Capricorn man is a woman who can show support for his decisions, listen to his thoughts, and agree to his opinions. Nevertheless, he will want a woman who has her own principles, too. He will feel secure that he has a strong person on his side, someone that he can rely on.

Step 3: Don't Smother Him

The best way to let a Capricorn man reach his potentials in life is to give him room to breathe. The Capricorn is an achiever, a go-getter. Naturally, he will need his own space to move around and time to do some thinking. By now, you should be aware that this guy is a planner. So don't hug all of his time and don't expect him to spend every minute with you. Some Capricorn men who feel smothered in their relationships will pull away. If the woman is not aware of the personality traits of the Capricorn guy, she might misunderstand this behavior and it can cause relationship problems.

Chapter 5: The Best Zodiac Matches for the Capricorn

After learning all about the Capricorn man – his personality traits, how to make him fall in love, and how to create a lasting relationship with him, it would seem that the Capricorn male is a handful. Among the Zodiacs, the Capricorn male is the most ambitious, most focused, and consequently, has the biggest chance to succeed in life. Because of his nature, the Capricorn man will need a woman who can support him and stand by him as he works to attain his dreams.

Intrigued by the Capricorn man? Wondering if you are a good match for him? Well wonder no more because here are the best matches for the Capricorn male according to astrological calculations.

The Most Compatible Mates for the Capricorn Male

Scorpio

The Scorpio woman is considered the most compatible match for the Capricorn male. These two will connect harmoniously on emotional and sexual levels. Nevertheless, the Capricorn male is often more dominant in the relationship and this can be a problem for the assertive Scorpio woman. If the Scorpio woman can adjust to this trait of the Capricorn man, then these two are the perfect match.

Virgo

The compatibility of the Capricorn with the Virgo lies in their both being intelligent. They connect intellectually making it easy to talk to each other. They are hard workers and both yearn for financial and career stability. The Capricorn and the Virgo are also sexually compatible. The Virgo can be headstrong at times, and that can feel threatening for the Capricorn.

Taurus

The Taurus woman is suitable to a Capricorn male because they are both practical. They both have goals and they enjoy planning for the future. In general, the Capricorn man will have problems treating his partner as an equal. However, with a Taurus woman, he can easily accept her as an equal. She has dreams and ambitions like him and she works hard like him. Although it seems like a match made in heaven, both possess a strong nature and that can be a problem in some cases. If they learn to compromise, then the relationship could be a successful one.

Other Possible Matches

Capricorn

A Capricorn woman can also make a suitable mate for the Capricorn man because they are alike in all ways. The problem is that they are too much alike that there is a risk that chemistry is lost. They become like business partners, companions, and even friends, not lovers. They tend to become too focused in the achievement of their goals that they neglect to make time for love and their relationship.

Pisces

The Pisces woman is a suitable match with the Capricorn man because she admires and respects him. He, on the other hand, enjoys being looked up to. The Pisces is very devoted and she makes a perfect match for the loyal Capricorn. The combination of their almost opposite personality traits create a balance in their relationship.

Libra

The Libra woman seems to be a good partner for the Capricorn man. She sheds light and positivity to the negativity of the Capricorn. Libras are happy-go-lucky, adventurous, and romantic people – the opposite of Capricorns. These two can form a potentially happy and successful relationship.

It may seem difficult to find a suitable match for the Capricorn man but really, all this man needs is a woman who understands him. And once you know about the personality traits of the Capricorn male, it's easy to determine whether you can be a good match for him or not.

Conclusion

Romantics believe that somewhere out there is the right person for everyone. All we need to do is to find our perfect counterpart. But how do we know who our most suitable matches are? Knowledge of Astrology and the Zodiac signs have provided some clues for us, giving us an idea about which signs can be compatible with each other.

Finding the right man for you can be as simple as looking at the Zodiac signs. If you have a Capricorn man in your sight, this is the time to find out whether he can be the right guy for you. Through this book, we hope that you've gotten a clear idea about the personality traits of the Capricorn man, how to get him to notice you, how to make him fall in love with you, and how to have a meaningful and lasting relationship.

Do keep in mind that the use of Astrology and Zodiac signs as a guideline in searching for true love is only one among many. It should not be used as the primary basis for creating and maintaining romantic relationships. If you are in love with a Capricorn man or if you think that the Capricorn man is the right guy for you, then by all means, get to know him better and allow him to get to know the real you. The magic that happens between people who are truly compatible with each other is not dictated by the stars but by the heart.

Finally, I'd like to thank you for purchasing this book! If you enjoyed it or found it helpful, I'd greatly appreciate it if you'd take a moment to leave a review on Amazon. Thank you!

Printed in Great Britain
by Amazon